TAKE MY DATE PLEASE!

REAL LIFE DATING DISASTERS

RICH WIENER

PUBLISHED BY FIDELI PUBLISHING INC.

TAKE MY DATE PLEASE!
REAL LIFE DATING DISASTERS

©Copyright 2013, Richard W. Wiener

All Rights Reserved.

No part of this book may be reproduced, stored in electronic format, or transmitted without written permission from the author.

ISBN: 978-1-60414-650-9

Fideli Publishing Inc.
119 W. Morgan St.
Martinsville, IN 46151

www.FideliPublishing.com

DEDICATION

This book is dedicated to anyone and everyone who has had a date from hell or a strange experience while on a date. It makes no difference what color, age, or nationality you are, as dating is still dating.

TABLE OF CONTENTS

Dedication .... *iii*
Foreword .... *vii*
Preface .... *ix*

Take Me Home 1
The Ride From Hell 4
Surprise Surprise 7
Here Come The Judge 9
Off To The Health Club 11
Crying 13
The Clown 16
The Drooler 19
The Blue Pill 21
The Artist 24
Bowling Anyone? 26
Sex After Marriage 29
The Timeshare 32
Sister Act 35
Just Unbelievable 39
Facebook 43
Never Satisfied 47
The Outhouse 51
That Darn Back Pocket 55
Are You For Real? 58
Not In The Shrubs 61
The Wooden Leg 64
Body Odor 67

Busted	70
The Trunk	74
The Dog	76
Seasick	78
Drunk	82
It Only Takes One	86
Epilogue	89
About The Author	91

FOREWORD

No matter if you live in the United States or Russia, in Canada or on the Moon, dating is the same. Online dating is the way to go for most people. There are loads of good stories, but there are also many horror stories. Most people have had at least one date that they would like to forget.

Relationships are extremely difficult in your later years, as everyone has some kind of baggage. Baggage can be as small as a wallet or as large as a trunk, but it is still baggage. Over the years, men and women become set in their ways and look for specific things from a partner. Some people are very flexible, and some are not.

If you have read Check Please..& Hurry! you would have seen the dark, but often funny, side of dating. What you are about to read are more stories from the dark side plus realistic views from the author Richard W. Wiener, the dating guru.

As in Check Please..& Hurry!, the stories are true but no real names are used. More than three hundred men and women were interviewed and the best — or in this case, the worst — dates are in this book. After reading this book, you will know why you are telling anyone who will listen to Take My Date Please!

PREFACE

The experiences that I have had looking for the right relationship have inspired me to write a sequel to my first book, Check Please...& Hurry!

When men and women found out that I was writing a book about dates that went wrong, they wanted to tell me their stories. I have heard dating stories that I couldn't believe. When I was married, I never knew of the things that went on in the single dating world. You must have a sense of humor to survive.

Don't get me wrong; there are many more good dates than bad dates, and some people I interviewed never had a bad date. But those who had bad dates seemed like they could recall every moment of those dates.

Don't let the bad dates that you will read about in this book discourage you. They have not deterred me from finding my last date.

TAKE ME HOME

Mae was really excited to finally go on a date with Harold. They'd been corresponding over the Internet for more than a month, and then on the phone for another month. Neither one of them wanted to move too fast, and they wanted to get to know each other before the actual meeting.

Mae was 53, and looked even younger than her posted photo. She was in good shape, as her way of life included six days a week at the health club, plus a yoga class. She'd been married for a short time, and had no children. She was a lab tech, which gave her a decent income.

Harold, on the other hand, had been married twice and had two grown children. He was 55 and balding, but was in decent shape himself, according to his photo and profile.

Because they'd spoken for hours over a period of time, Mae felt comfortable having Harold pick her up at her condo. She lived in a building with a doorman, and her guests had to be announced before they could be sent up to the fifth floor.

Mae had a vision of Harold as a good-looking, successful businessman with class and charm. Her gut was telling her that this man had potential for a long relationship.

Her phone rang and Hugo the doorman told her she had a guest in the lobby. Harold was right on time. He'd said he would pick her up at eight, and it was exactly eight. Mae was thrilled, as being late was one of the pet peeves she had told him about during one of their conversations. There was no need for Harold to come up, so she told Hugo to tell him she would be right down.

When the elevator door opened, Harold was standing in the lobby looking out the window. When he turned around, he looked quite different from his picture. He was maybe five years older and a few pounds heavier, and was completely bald rather than balding.

Mae felt disappointed, but she was determined to have a nice evening out. After all, she had invested two months of emailing and talking. How bad could this evening be?

His car was parked in the driveway. She did a double take, as she had not seen a Pinto in years. A green one, no less. Plus, she was feeling overdressed in a skirt and blouse when he was wearing jeans. The back seat held old coffee cups and a few empty Coke cans. She wasn't expecting this based on their conversations.

Being a positive person was all that kept her from screaming. And the evening was just beginning.

Now what did he have in mind for dinner? They couldn't be going somewhere nice with Harold dressed like that. And she was soooo right.

He pulled up to a Chinese restaurant and, instead of leaving the Pinto with the valet, he drove around looking for a space on the street. After four spins around the block, he found a tight spot but the Pinto fit right in it. Luckily the weather was nice, as the walk was not short. He hadn't thought to drop her off before parking.

It was Saturday night, so anyone without a reservation had to wait. Well guess what? They had no reservation. The wait was around 30 minutes.

Harold told Mae that this was his favorite restaurant, and he knew the menu blindfolded. It was about 9:30 when their pager started flashing. She was famished, and couldn't wait to eat.

When the waiter was ready to take their orders, Harold took the liberty of ordering for both of them. He ordered some kind of surprise duck and noodles. Mae had wanted egg foo young, but didn't want to upset Harold. He was absolutely sure she would like what he'd ordered. Again she wanted to scream.

She was having a hard time being nice. She just wanted to eat and go home. She didn't even like their conversation, and she was feeling like she wasted two months on this man. He was nice on the phone, but in person he was just plain obnoxious!

When the check came, she even offered to split it. He told her she could leave the tip. Again, she wanted to scream. Now the conversation was one sided, as she didn't even want to talk. He had no clue, and had mentioned going to a movie on their next date. *Next date my ass,* she thought.

She could hardly wait to get away from him. She knew that if her friends were in this situation they would've left and called a cab, but being mean wasn't easy for her.

On the ride back to her condo, he mentioned that maybe he could come up for a glass of wine. She didn't say anything, but thought, *That will happen when pigs fly!*

About six blocks from her house, she heard a police siren. The police actually pulled the Pinto over for a broken taillight. Finally out of character, she jumped out of the car and told the police officer to put her in the back of the squad car. She told him that she was on the date from hell and asked if he would drive her home. Otherwise, she was walking.

It must have startled the doorman when she got out of the back of a police car. She thanked the officer profusely for saving her. When she opened the door to her condo, she let out a loud scream.

THE RIDE FROM HELL

Nancy couldn't wait for her date with Nolan. She hadn't been on a date for a few months and seemed to hit it off with him, even though she hadn't met him face to face. He contacted her through a dating site and told her he was interested and, if she found him interesting, to contact him.

After reading his profile and looking at his photo, she wrote him and left her cell number in the message. He was 6'3" and had what appeared to be a good build. He had never been married, and owned a small business.

Nancy had been married for 16 years, and her divorce had become final a year earlier. She was ready to get out there again and get it right this time. At 50 years old, she had many good years left, and wanted to spend them with the right man.

Nolan lived about 20 miles away and told her he had a special date planned, one that she would always remember. He wouldn't tell her where they were going, only that this would be the best first date she'd ever have.

Nancy was excited and wanted to make a great first impression. She had long, beautiful hair and made an appointment at her salon for a wash and blowout. She also had a mani/pedi while she was there. When she walked out of the salon, she looked great and felt even better.

She thought long and hard about what to wear. It would've helped if he'd given her even a clue about where they were going. What a dilemma. She decided to wear a black miniskirt and a red blouse. When she looked at herself in the mirror, she thought she'd be in love if she was a man.

Her friends thought she was crazy for letting a strange man pick her up without telling her where they were going. They tried talking her out of it, but she wouldn't budge. She wanted to have fun and was the type of person who took chances and lived on the edge.

Nolan was to pick her up at six. He arrived at her house about 15 minutes late, as traffic wasn't cooperating with him. When Nancy opened the door to greet him, she was satisfied with the way he looked, but not how he was dressed. He had on a pair of jeans and a denim shirt. She was too much of a lady to make any comment to him.

After closing the front door of her house, however, she stopped in her tracks. He didn't have a car. He had a motorcycle! He told her they were running late and had to leave right away in order to get to where he was taking her. He then handed her a helmet to put on over her beautiful head of hair.

If she had it to do over again, she would've at least put on a pair of jeans. Sitting on the back of a motorcycle in a miniskirt was very breezy. Not only that, but her skirt kept crawling up her thighs.

He was flying in and out of traffic on the freeway. Nancy almost peed her pants with fear. It was hot outside, and she was sweating profusely under the helmet. She knew she'd look like a drowned rat when she took it off. She somehow held in her disapproval, but couldn't wait to get back to the safety of her home.

They drove about an hour to their destination. He was taking her to a country and western concert. He never even asked her if she liked that type of music, which she didn't.

The concert lasted about two hours. After looking around, she knew she was really overdressed. Everyone had on jeans, and many men were wearing shit-kicking boots.

She finally spoke up as they were leaving, telling Nolan that he had a lot of nerve planning this date without telling her. She told him she would've dressed differently had she known where they were going, and that she didn't like motorcycles or country and western music.

She also told him that if he was planning on taking the freeway back home she would be taking a cab, and didn't care what it cost. The trip home via side streets took an hour and a half. It seemed like days to Nancy. When the motorcycle pulled up in front of her house, she jumped off, took off her helmet, and threw it at him. She couldn't believe it when Nolan asked her if she was going to ask him in.

She looked at him with daggers in her eyes and told him to get on his bike and never contact her again. She ended the evening by telling Nolan that, thanks to him, she had now been on *the* date from hell.

SURPRISE! SURPRISE!

Jack was so looking forward to his second date with Millie. Their first date was quite nice. They had a quiet dinner with a bottle of wine and great conversation. He felt that they were really getting to know all about each other.

They'd met at a party thrown by a mutual friend to celebrate the opening of an art studio. Jack noticed this attractive girl looking at a piece he thought was a bunch of paint just thrown on a canvas. She seemed really engrossed in this painting.

Jack approached her and said, "What a neat piece of work." Millie turned and smiled at him. He had to put on a good act, as he didn't know jack shit about art.

Playing the perfect gentleman, he asked if she would like a drink. He was quite interested in her. Why shouldn't he be? She was good looking, and had curves where they belonged.

Jack thought she had an interest in him, too, so he stepped up his game plan and asked her to dinner. He didn't notice a ring on her finger, so he decided to go for it. She accepted his invitation and they set a date for the following Saturday night.

Millie met him at the restaurant and the evening was perfect. He was feeling great as, for the first time in a long time, he'd met someone who wasn't from a dating site. He didn't even have to wait for the evening to end to ask to see her again, because she invited him to her home the following week. This was too good to be true.

The night of their second meeting, he stopped and picked up some flowers. He even had a glass of wine before he left his apartment to celebrate his newfound interest.

Millie lived in a rather large house. It had a circular driveway that could hold around twelve cars. When he pulled up, he parked behind two cars that were already in the driveway. She had a three-car garage, and one garage door was open, with a sports car in it. Jack was feeling curious as to who owned these nice cars.

As he walked up to the front door, he noticed several people moving around through the shaded-glass window. Maybe she was having some friends over for dinner. He rang the doorbell. When she opened the front door, his jaw dropped at what he saw.

She was wearing a bathrobe, and so were her guests— two other men. Her eyes appeared glassy, like she was on something. He wasn't curious enough to get an explanation. With flowers in hand, he just turned around and headed back to his car. He wouldn't have believed it if he hadn't seen it. What was she into?

On his drive back home, he knew that this was too good to be true. He mentally beat himself up. He knew connecting with this beautiful young woman and actually having a relationship was too goo to be true. He learned a valuable lesson — don't think too far ahead and get excited too early in the relationship. His started thinking about what had just happened. She was a young woman living in a large house. The house was expensive, and she was a legal secretary. Legal secretaries didn't make enough to afford a house like that. She was probably going to use him for something, but he would never find out what. Back to the Internet.

HERE COMES THE JUDGE

Julie was excited about her date, a distinguished-looking man she met online who said he was in his mid-60s. Julie herself was in her mid-50s, and did not mind the age difference. She had dated older men before, and found them very charming.

He made the first contact, and Julie responded immediately. He did not want to spend time emailing and would rather have a phone conversation. She also preferred that, so they exchanged phone numbers.

They spoke two times, and then decided to make a date to meet face to face. Julie preferred to meet for lunch. He was a judge, so he had to look at his schedule to see when he would be free. They decided on a day the following week.

He picked the restaurant, which was near the downtown courthouse. He told her that he would meet her there at 12:30, and that he would make reservations. She left it all up to him, as she felt a judge would have more pull than she would.

When she arrived around 12:15, she waited for the judge in the bar area. The restaurant he picked was quite a popular place, full of attorneys and businessmen. She ordered a glass of merlot and patiently waited, looking for a six-foot-tall man with greying hair and a grey beard.

At exactly 12:30, she noticed a man enter the restaurant. He looked nothing like the photo she had seen on the computer. Her pictures were very current and could not be mistaken. Within seconds, this man of around 70 walked up to her and hugged her hello. She was in total shock. He was wearing a suit that must have come from Robert Hall around 30 years ago. She was dressed quite sexily, wearing a shorter-than-average black skirt with black, high-top boots. She felt eyes looking at her, and hoped people did not think she was a hooker or a woman with a sugar daddy. She actually thought about leaving, but figured she might as well have lunch with him, even if she had no desire to see him again.

They were seated in a semi-round booth, and were too close for her liking. The judge ordered a bottle of wine without asking her if she would like another glass of what she was drinking.

She was dying to ask him why he lied on the computer and how old his pictures were, but decided to just let it go, have lunch, and leave. They were making small talk when he took his right hand and placed it on her inner left thigh, only a few inches from the promised land.

Julie jumped up and out of the booth. In a rather loud voice, she asked him, "Why did you touch me?" Noticing everyone looking at this scene, the judge was actually speechless and just looked at her. She preceded to call him an "old pig" and walked out of the restaurant at an Olympic pace.

While driving home, she hoped that she would never have to go to court with him on the bench. By touching her where he did, he gave another meaning to "here comes the judge!"

OFF TO THE HEALTH CLUB

"Oh my lord, I'm single and have to get myself in shape if I'm going to meet someone." That cry is familiar for men and women who have become single after years of marriage because they're now divorced or widowed. Many people in marriages become very complacent and don't really notice their appearance. We all change over the years. How many people look at their wedding pictures and don't recognize themselves anymore? People have no trouble being naked with their husband or wife, but the thought of undressing in front of a new man or woman can cause chills in most people.

The key word in getting back out in the single world is "marketable!" How can a man be marketable with a huge stomach that hangs over his belt? How can a woman be marketable with an ass that can hardly fit into a chair? Now panic starts to seep in.

Weight Watchers and Jenny Craig are full of newly single people. Along with the growing membership in these weight-loss centers comes the rising in health club memberships. Thank goodness for Spandex. How many married people do you think have an exercise wardrobe in their closet if they never worked out before? Probably none.

Being single costs a lot of money. The weight-loss program, the health club membership, and the workout wardrobe. Did you ever notice what people wear to the health club? An older man should never wear Spandex shorts. An older woman with a rather large backside should never, ever wear flower-patterned Spandex shorts. The flowers on her ass turn into a garden. Just check yourself out in the mirror, or have a friend critique your outfit.

It is very interesting that I see men and women working out who appear to be getting bigger and not lighter. I do realize that it is very difficult to lose weight as we get older. If exercise and diet do not work, you might have to figure out a different routine or hire a personal trainer — maybe even see a nutritionist to educate yourself on the proper foods to eat.

Maybe you think that by working out you can indulge in your favorite foods. After a good workout one day, I went out for a bite to eat. At another table were two women who I had noticed at the club. They were of the larger variety, needing to drop maybe 50 pounds each. I couldn't help but notice what they were consuming. cheeseburgers and french fries, with shakes to wash it all down. Some people are entirely hopeless.

Not everyone is like that, as I have seen many men and women become very "marketable" by changing their lives around. I used to think that there is someone for everyone, but I do not think that anymore.

CRYING

Annie, like most young women, wanted to find her perfect match. She was smart enough to know that was like finding a needle in a haystack. But she felt that she was different from most of her friends, as she would give just about any man a chance. Her friends were into looks, but she felt that if a man had a good personality, it would make up for the looks part.

She had been divorced for three years and had no children, so her baggage was quite minimal. She knew she would make a good partner in a relationship. The only problem was finding her other half.

Her dates came from dating sites, being fixed up, or just meeting someone at a bar or grocery store. She was an average-looking woman with a very outgoing personality. She would go on about five dates a month.

One evening the phone rang, and it was her aunt. After exchanging the usual pleasantries, her aunt proceeded to tell her about her friend's son, who had become widowed about a year ago and was just beginning to go out.

The description her aunt gave was very interesting. He was in his 40s, owned his own business, and was nice looking. He lived in a high-end highrise, and had no children. Everything that Annie was told was very positive and interesting. She was sure that her aunt wouldn't fix her up with an undesirable.

Before they hung up, Annie gave her aunt permission to give out her phone number. She always liked when someone asked permission before giving out her number.

He called a couple days later, and they had a rather nice conversation. Annie was careful not to ask too many questions about his late wife during their first conversation.

Since her aunt knew him, she decided it was alright to have dinner with him on the first date. Usually it was just coffee on a first meeting, but this was different.

Harry's was a nice steakhouse that both of them liked. They would meet there for dinner at 7:30. He made a reservation, which was needed at this very popular restaurant.

Annie arrived a few minutes early, and waited in the bar area. Because she didn't know what he looked like, they arranged to call each other while in the bar area so they could find each other. Annie ordered a glass of wine and waited for his call.

While she was waiting, a man with terrible breath was hitting on her. She was trying to be nice, but he had smoker's breath with bad garlic mixed in. She was starting to gag when her cell rang. Thank God she did not have to smell that putrid breath anymore.

He was standing about 15 feet away when he called her. He was a nice-looking man with a decent build. Her aunt was right about his looks. She knew how people could exaggerate about such things, especially when it involved a friend's son.

The conversation was normal. Annie still avoided asking about his late wife, but knew it was coming when he started talking about his life. She saw that he was becoming a little emotional. About 10 minutes into the conversation, he completely broke down and couldn't stop crying. She did not know what to do, as she was getting embarrassed. He was not ready to date. She could strangle her aunt.

Everyone was looking at them, and she did not know what to do; she had never been in a situation like this. Finally, when he calmed down, she asked the waiter for the check. She just wanted to leave. After composing himself, he paid the check and they headed out. She thanked him for dinner and headed for her car.

She knew that there were certain people you do not go out with: people who are recently divorced, widowed, or separated. She would go on to live by that rule. She would not have gone on that date if it wasn't for her dear old aunt. The next time her aunt called and she saw the name on the caller ID, she would not answer.

THE CLOWN

After two weeks of emailing and talking on the phone, Fred was all set to meet Lois. He noticed her on Match.com and sent her a short email telling her that he was interested. He was used to not getting a response back. If he had a quarter for everyone he emailed and never got a response from, he could take a small vacation.

He could not believe his eyes when she responded, telling him that she was also interested. He immediately emailed her his cell number and waited for her to call.

He did not have to wait too long, as she called him within 10 minutes of his email. Maybe his luck was starting to change. He had been on Match for three years, and knew that finding the right girl was a numbers game. Maybe his number was up. He knew better than to get too excited, as he had been disappointed many times before, but he always tried to stay positive.

He liked the way she looked. She had long, red hair with what he could tell from her photo was a decent figure. He was in good shape and went to the health club religiously. He just knew that he would not disappoint her.

They knew quite a lot about each other from their long phone conversations. Lois had been married twice, as had Fred.

Both had three children. Fred was a sports fanatic, and Lois liked basketball and baseball. When they would meet, they would not have to talk about the things people normally do on a first meeting. Very similar to a job interview. Fred hated first meetings. Most of them were one and done.

Since they seemed to know each other just by talking, he decided to take her to dinner instead of the usual coffee meeting. Lois also liked the idea of dinner. She even told him that he could pick her up at her house. She was breaking her major rule about having a man know where she lived before meeting face to face.

On the way to her home, Fred was getting nervous. What if she did not look like her picture? After all, they were taken from a distance. Well, it was past the point of no return.

Fred was right on time. He did not like to be late, and hated people who were always late. It was exactly eight when he rang the doorbell. He had his fingers crossed as he heard footsteps coming to open the door.

When she opened the door, he froze in amazement. Lois had a very good figure. She looked great from the shoulders down — but her face! She must have had stock in Revlon, as she wore tons of make-up. She reminded him of Tammy Faye Baker. She also had on bright-red lipstick that made her mouth look like a target.

If he could, he would have excused himself and gotten the hell out of Dodge. But Fred was a gentleman, and carried out the dinner plans. He had to restrain himself from breaking into laughter every time he looked at her. Her clown face was just like the ones in the circus; he wanted to drive her to Ringling Brothers.

The restaurant was crowded, and he had his fingers crossed that he would not see anyone he knew. Didn't anyone ever mention to her that she did not need so much make-up? He was not curious to see what was behind that mask. Maybe it was Jimmy Hoffa or Elvis.

At least the dinner was excellent. He wanted to eat and run, but she seemed to be having a good time. It was 9:30, and the restaurant had a band that started playing in the lounge area.

Fred noticed that many people were taking second glances at Lois. If he was not with her, he would probably do the same. He kept looking at his watch when she was not looking at him.

The band was playing rock music, but then played a slow song and invited all the couples to the dance floor. Lois looked Fred in the eye and asked him to dance with her. So he obliged, and off to the dance floor they went. Fred was wearing a navy-blue, cashmere sweater, and almost crapped in his pants when Lois put her head on his shoulder. She left half her face on his beautiful sweater.

After the dance, he excused himself and headed for the men's room. When he looked at himself in the mirror, he just about died. His sweater was loaded with her make-up. He just wanted to leave.

He was sure that she noticed his sweater, but never mentioned a word. Fred could not take it anymore, and told her that he was not feeling well and that they should leave. The ride home was very quiet.

The next day, when his friends called him to ask about his date, all he would say was he had gone out with Bozo!

THE DROOLER

Freda could not wait to meet Wally face to face. They connected on a dating site, and she was blown away by his posted pictures. His features were very appealing to her, and she considered herself a woman of good taste.

She had a good job as a life coach, with a large client base. Her marriage had lasted only a few years, as her ex-husband was an alcoholic and very abusive. Being a professional woman, she wasn't about to hang around and hope that he would change.

Now she was a free woman and determined not to make the same mistake with her judgement in finding the right man. She was very outgoing, and knew she was the complete package.

She put herself on a dating site and devoted an hour to it each night. She received many emails, which she knew she would. Most of the time, she would hit the delete button. If the posted photos were not to her liking, she moved on to the next one.

When she saw Wally on the site, she was interested and emailed him back telling him that she liked his look and asked how recent the pictures were. She did not like to be fooled by dishonest men. Her posted photos were quite recent, taken at a wedding she attended two months earlier.

Wally assured her that his pictures were not more than six months old. He told her that he had been fooled many times himself. He asked if she would like to meet for a drink of a cup of coffee.

In most cases, Freda would like to talk on the phone before any face-to-face meeting. Whatever got into her, she decided in this case she would meet for a drink at the bar in a nearby hotel.

She was very flexible about the time, since she made her own hours. Wally owned a printing company, so he was not as flexible. He told her that he would like to go home first to change clothes, and asked if seven was fine with her. So the meeting was set.

Freda arrived first, sat at a high-top table, and ordered a glass of pinot. If he indeed looked like his picture, she would notice him immediately.

Fifteen minutes was all she had to wait, as she noticed a nice-looking man walking into the bar. She raised her arm so he would notice her, which he did.

They exchanged the usual pleasantries and he sat down. He ordered a vodka on the rocks and told her that she looked better than her pictures.

After a few minutes, she noticed something. When he talked, he drooled! He would drool from each side of his mouth, and kept wiping it. This was very annoying, as he could not get a sentence out without dripping from his mouth. She knew that this was a one and done. She was thinking that if she kissed him, she would need a life vest to keep from drowning.

She had never heard of such a thing, and was not going to ask about it. The hour she spent watching him drool seemed like an eternity.

After an hour, she told him that she did not think they were a match. She wondered if she would have noticed something in his speech if they talked on the phone? She did learn a lesson, as this was the last time she would meet someone without speaking to them on the phone first.

THE BLUE PILL

Inez had a wonderful first date with Mitch. They connected at a wedding of a mutual friend. They were next to each other in line at the bar, waiting to order drinks. Mitch started the conversation, telling Inez how beautiful she looked. She returned the compliment, and they continued talking well after they left the bar area.

The rest of the evening they danced, drank, and flirted. It so happened that both were dateless for the wedding, which worked out well. Mitch left his table to squeeze into hers. He didn't even know who he was sitting with.

They talked about everything from politics to their personal lives. He was divorced with one son, and she was divorced with one daughter. They both had good jobs. She was a real-estate broker, and he owned a printing business. He lived in the city, and she the suburbs. They both loved the movies and the theatre.

Inez definitely felt a connection, and knew Mitch did too. She enjoyed being held tight during the slow dances. Mitch even kissed her cheek a few times. On one occasion, they walked out of the ballroom and, when no one was around, they engaged in some tonsil hockey. He was holding her close, and she could detect his happiness.

Before they left, they exchanged contact information, and Mitch told her that he would call her to make plans. He could not wait to continue where they left off. She gave him the message that she also wanted more. He wanted to have sex with her in the worst way. He would not wait too long to call.

Actually, he called her the next day to make plans. He asked her if she wouldn't mind driving into the city, as his car was in the shop. She saw nothing wrong with that, and trusted him after spending several hours with him at the wedding.

She wrote down the directions he gave her, and the plan was to pick him up at eight on Saturday night. He told her that he had a surprise for her, and she liked surprises. Maybe play tickets or a nice restaurant.

Saturday night, she left her suburban home at 7:15. She thought that would give her ample time to get to his place. The problem was that the traffic going into the city was bumper to bumper. She would never get to his place by eight, and was getting very nervous. She called to tell him, and he sounded a little upset. Maybe he had theater tickets and they would be late. She was getting more and more aggravated, and started cussing out the other drivers for not moving.

It took her two hours to reach her destination. She parked her car and headed for the elevator. She hoped that he was not too upset with her.

When he opened the door, he was wearing a bathrobe. The door wasn't even closed before he started kissing her. She felt this huge thing while he was kissing her. He started steering her to the bedroom. What was his hurry? She had no intention of sleeping with him so soon. She pushed him away and said she had to use the bathroom. While in the bathroom, she noticed a bottle of Viagra. She started putting two and two together. She heard that it only lasted for four hours; he must have taken it much earlier and was afraid that it would expire.

She could hear him telling her to speed it up. She was thinking how to get out of there. She yelled for him to wait for her in the bedroom, and said she would be right out.

When she opened the door and noticed the coast was clear, she hightailed it out the door and did not wait for the elevator, thinking that he would follow her out. She walked down to the next floor and hit the button.

She learned a valuable lesson — never go to a man's home on the first date. She knew that she would have to be smarter in the future. She was liking him and felt a connection, but did not want to be connected to him so soon.

THE ARTIST

While surfing Match.com on her computer, Lola noticed a man she might be interested in. He was good looking, and he was an artist and photographer. She read through his entire profile and decided to take a chance. She sent him an email, hoping that he would have interest in her.

She did not have to wait too long, as she received an immediate reply. He must have been online at the same time she was. His name was John, and he had been an artist his entire working life. He sent his cell number in his response, and told her that he would rather talk than email. She was on the same page.

She was interested in art, and had several nice pieces of art in her home. John sent her pictures of some of his work. After seeing what he sent her, she knew he was very talented.

They lived close to each other, and John invited her over to his house, which doubled as his gallery. Lola had a rule about going over to someone's house before really knowing them, but she decided to take a chance.

The ride over was very short, maybe 10 minutes. She parked in front and looked at his house. It looked kind of seedy. It was poorly maintained, and it looked like the Addams Family might have lived there. She didn't want to judge a book by its cover, because she knew artists were of a different nature.

She rang the bell and he came to the door, totally looking the part of an artist. His clothes were paint stained, and he even had some paint on his cheek. She just wanted to see his work and get out.

He was a hoarder. She had heard about hoarders, but never met one before. He had more junk in his house than she had ever seen before. He had newspapers that must have been from World War II. She noticed a few roaches who looked quite comfortable in these surroundings. The musty smell was nauseating, and the dust must have been two inches thick.

Lola never made it to the gallery in the house, not even caring to see his work. She abruptly turned and was heading for the door when jumped in front of her, wanting to steal a kiss. He grabbed her but, before he could open his mouth, she gave him a swift knee in his family jewels. The last she saw of him, he was hunched over in pain. She almost tripped over what looked like a bedpan on her way out.

BOWLING ANYONE?

Dennis wanted his first date with Rose to be different, so he wanted to plan an activity. He had been talking to Rose for a few weeks, but they were never able to coordinate their busy schedules.

He mentioned to her about going bowling. Rose was not much of a bowler, but figured it would be a good idea because they would be in a crowded place for their first actual meeting. Even though she had not been to a bowling alley in more than twenty years, she thought this might be fun.

She didn't really have a feel for Dennis. They'd had nice conversations about the usual things, like family and life in general. She'd met some nice men on dating sites, and never really had a bad experience.

They arranged to meet in the foyer of the Brunswick lanes bowling alley near her home. She had no intention of letting him pick her up on a first date. She did not have to drive more than ten minutes, which was even better.

They arranged to meet in the foyer of the bowling alley. They arrived within three minutes of each other. Both of them looked exactly like their posted pictures.

Of course, Rose did not own a bowling ball or shoes. Dennis had his own shiny ball, and shoes to match. He was ready to show off his wonderful ability. Rose could care less.

Dennis was a very competitive person and hated losing at anything. He was like a child who never grew up. She would find this out very early in the game.

Rose had a hard time keeping her ball from going into the gutter. As a matter of fact, she had seven gutter balls after the first six frames. Dennis, meanwhile, did not pay much attention to Rose at all. He was concentrating on getting another strike. He had a perfect game going through six frames.

In the seventh frame, disaster fell upon them. Rose accidentally dropped her ball on top of her foot, and fell in extreme pain. As soon as she hit the ground, Dennis let out a loud, "Oh shit!" Rose didn't know if it was because she was hurt or because of loosing the chance at his perfect score. Dennis helped her up and just about carried her to the bench. By that time, everyone around them was coming over to offer help.

Dennis seemed quite upset with Rose for ruining his game. Her foot was swelling up like a balloon, but Dennis didn't say a word. Someone must have called an ambulance, as three paramedics came to her aid. After looking at her foot, they suggested taking her to the hospital to have it X-rayed, as they could not tell if it was broken because of all the swelling.

Dennis followed the ambulance to the hospital and waited with her. He had very little to say, except to keep asking her how she dropped the ball. After a while, she just wanted him to leave.

They were in the waiting area for more than three hours, and Rose finally told Dennis that he did not have to stay with her. She didn't have to tell him twice, as he left without saying a word.

She was more relaxed with him gone. She could not believe what an asshole this man was. The only thought in her mind was what would have happened if she'd hurt her foot in the last frame, when he was one strike away from perfection.

SEX AFTER MARRIAGE

I'm sure the title of this chapter will grab your attention. It would surely grab mine. After all, sex is one of the main topics of discussion no matter one's age, color, or nationality. When you are dating someone, the topic of sex will eventually come up.

It is easier, in most cases, for a man than a woman. I am sure some women will debate that statement. After a divorce, it is easier for a man to go out and date. The women simply outnumber the men by a wide margin.

A woman who has been in a long marriage and has had only one sexual partner finds being with another man very strange and, in the beginning, quite uncomfortable. That is only before her first encounter. Once the ice has been broken, then it becomes much easier the next time, and the time after that.

No matter how old a person is, once those juices start flowing, you feel like a teenager all over again. In some marriages, sex has disappeared. Once those marriages end, it takes a little time for that urge to return. But the good news is it will.

The most difficult part of sex with a new partner is being naked in front of them. You certainly don't look like you did 20, 30, or 40 years ago. This is one of the main reasons men and women flock to health clubs to try to get those bodies into some kind of decent shape. If you took a survey and asked men and women if they prefer having sex with the lights on or off, the answer would be off. My suggestion is to try candlelight. Much more romantic than a dark room.

Another big decision is how many dates to go on with the same person before you decide to have sex. The answer varies from couple to couple. I know a woman who has a three-month rule; she has to be dating a man for at least three months before jumping in the sack with him.

On the other hand, I know a woman who has a three-date rule. Some men have their rules too, like a three-hour rule. One dating site asks women how many dates they would go on with the same man before they would have sex with him. A good majority of the answers said six or more dates. When it asked the men the same question, the majority said one or two dates. There is no right answer. It all depends on the chemistry, and if it feels right.

A nurse who works in an emergency room once told me, "Do what you enjoy for as long as you can, because there will be a time when you cannot do it anymore." That is a powerful, but true, statement.

When I interviewed people for this book, many told me that sex was much better after marriage. The reason being that, after a period of time, sex in a marriage is not as important and each partner takes the other for granted. It is just plain missionary, if you get the drift. One important thing to remember is that the people interviewed were all divorced or widowed.

Sex after marriage becomes more experimental, as many divorced men and women said that they have experienced things that they didn't during their marriages. In other words, they are doing different things sexually, things that they had not experienced before. Let's just leave it at that.

So the consensus is that sex after marriage is something people would never expect. Whether you are divorced or widowed, it is the same. At first it can be intimidating but, in time, you will learn that life is way too short and you have to enjoy yourself.

THE TIMESHARE

Jamie was looking at her dating websites, as she usually did every evening. She was not having much luck. She was a receptionist for a doctor and found it hard to meet men, so she decided to try the Internet. She had a few dates, but most of them were one and done.

On a Wednesday evening, she logged on and received a message from a man named Joey. At 56, he was age-appropriate. She was 50 and did not lie about her age like she'd heard many women and men did. Joey was nice looking and clean shaven, which was what she liked.

His message was quite detailed. He was a mechanic who worked at Lexus, and had been married for 15 years but had no children. He went on to tell her that her profile caught his attention and that she had a look that he liked. He included his cell number and told her that the ball was in her court.

She liked that, as he gave her the option of continuing or just forgetting about him. She decided to call him. What did she have to lose? After all, men were not knocking down her door.

She dialed his number and, after three rings, he picked up his phone. He sounded normal, for what normal was. He talked intelligently, and she knew that a mechanic was usually a smart guy. He would have to be in order to fix newer cars.

They talked for about forty-five minutes and, before hanging up, they decided to go out on the following Saturday night. Joey told her that he would make the plans, which she liked. A man who took control was her kind of guy.

She asked him if he could pick her up at a nearby hotel where she would leave her car. She never let someone pick her up at home until maybe the third date, if it ever got that far. So, they set the time for 7:30. He told her to just dress casually.

On Saturday, Jamie arrived around 7:20 and parked in the lot, where there were not many cars. Joey asked her what she was driving so he would recognize her car. She told him she would be in a 2010 BMW.

Joey showed up right on time. He was driving a 1995 Chrysler, which should have given her some kind of clue. She did not want to be shallow and judge him, but why was he in a 17-year-old car when he could fix cars himself?

She was thinking about offering to drive, but she couldn't bring herself to do that. She'd just suck it up, as she did not want to appear snobby.

He looked a little older than his photo, and a little heavier. She knew his photo was not recent, but just let it be. She was very curious about his plans for the evening. What would she be surprised with next?

They went to a restaurant that he had not been to before, as he told her he liked trying new things. He'd chosen an Italian restaurant called Mombo's. It was a rather large place, and maybe half filled on a Saturday night, which was not a good sign.

Jamie ordered a veal dish, and he ordered a pasta dish. The food was just okay. When the bill came, she found out why he chose that particular restaurant. From his wallet, he pulled out a buy-one-get-one coupon. She thought that was unacceptable on the first date, but she wouldn't think of saying anything.

What happened next was a true first for her. He asked her if she had ever gone to a timeshare meeting. She told him no, and he told her that all they had to do was go listen to a speaker talk about a timeshare in Brazil. He would collect $200, which he offered to split with her.

She had no idea what to say, and went along with him. They sat and listened and saw pictures for over an hour and a half. When they were finished with the movie, the salesman put on the full-court press, and they had a hard time leaving. Finally,, seeing that they would not budge, the salesman begrudgingly gave them two $100 bills. Joey gave Jamie one of them.

This was one of the worst dates Jamie had ever been on, and she was hoping that he had no more surprises. It was around 10:45 and she was tired. She wanted to just get back to her car, go home, and forget about the whole evening.

Joey asked if she wanted to stop for a nightcap at the hotel bar, but she declined, telling him she was tired. She thought that he would have her pay, since he got her the $100.

When Joey dropped her at her car, he asked her out on another date. Mustering up enough courage, she politely told him she didn't think they were a good match, as the chemistry was just not there. She felt that if she said that earlier, she would have never seen any money.

So, it was back to the drawing board.

SISTER ACT

Harry was a pretty successful business owner who had been divorced for six years and was getting that itch to get out there and find a woman. He was on a dating website, but was not very active with it. Even though he paid semi-annually, he hardly ever went online to check out the women.

He owned a heating and air conditioning company, which kept him very busy. He had been married for 10 years and had a young daughter, who also took up much of his time. He was now at the point where he wanted to have someone in his life again, so he finally became active on the site.

It was a Friday night when he sat down at his computer and began the search. He noticed some of the same women who were on a few years earlier. He figured they probably thought the same thing about him.

After going over many profiles, he found a rather interesting woman who looked good and was age-appropriate. She had long, dark hair and a great smile. She was rather tall, 5'10", which was another plus as he was 6'3".

He just had to write her and hoped that she would answer, as his friends told him that the majority of women contacted never wrote back or acknowledged the contact.

He wrote a rather long email introducing himself, asked her to let him know if she would like to talk, and sent her his cell phone number. Then he just crossed his fingers and hoped that she would answer him.

Two days later, his cell phone rang. When he looked at the caller ID, there was no name, just a number. Before he answered, he knew it was the girl he had emailed.

Her name was Jodie. She told him she really liked his email, and that she had to call him after he put in the effort and time to write her. She had received many emails, but never one so thoughtful. She told him that she liked his profile and his picture, and asked him when the picture was taken.

He couldn't lie and told her that it was two years old, as he had not put up anything current. She said that hers was a few years old as well, but that she looked the same. She also mentioned that she felt she looked better in person and was very active. She played tennis three times a week, and regularly went to the health club.

Harry was getting excited, as the conversation was going really well. She was a talker, which he also liked. He hated to be the one who always carried the conversation, and enjoyed a woman who could hold her own.

They spoke for about an hour, getting all the initial talk that two people do when they speak for the first time. The basic stuff like family, work, and hobbies. Before hanging up, they decided that they should meet instead of doing more talking on the phone.

Harry lived in the suburbs and Jodie resided in the city. Since Harry's business was located in the city, he chose to meet her after work at a restaurant bar. The time was set for five, which was happy hour at most places. The excitement was mounting.

It took Harry about 20 minutes to get to the restaurant. He was 15 minutes early, so he sat at a table near the rear of the bar, ordered a vodka on the rocks, and started to unwind. He noticed two women sitting at a table, both wearing sunglasses and big, floppy hats. They appeared to be looking in his direction and talking to each other. Harry felt they were talking about him. He tried not looking at them, and wished more people would come into the bar area so these two would occupy themselves looking at someone else.

At five on the head, a tall woman walked in. He knew immediately it was Jodie. She looked different from her photo, as her hair was much shorter and she seemed taller than what she told him.

She walked over to him, held out her hand to introduce herself, and sat down. Something seemed different when she started talking. He could swear she was not the same woman he'd talked to on the phone.

She ordered a Manhattan and he had another vodka. He was feeling a little uncomfortable, as the more they spoke, the more he knew this was a different woman. She didn't look like a woman who worked out and played tennis.

He just had to ask, as he couldn't sit and listen anymore. He just asked her if she was the one he'd spoken to the other day. The woman he'd spoken with on the phone was a good talker, and their conversation had not been strained like this one was.

The truth was about to come out. Her name was Jackie, and she was Jodie's sister. It was not the first time the two of them tried to pull this off, with Jackie replacing Jodie. Jodie was always trying to help her sister get a date. Jodie would do all the talking on the phone, while Jackie just listened to the conversation so she could carry the ball when she met the man in person. It might have worked if they hadn't been so very different.

Harry felt used and was quite upset. This was not the girl he intended to meet. Did they really think they could pull this off? Maybe with some other schmuck. He stood up, took $40 out of his wallet, and dropped it on the table. Without saying another word, he stormed out.

JUST UNBELIEVABLE

Iris heard many stories from her friends about their bad dates. She'd never really had what she considered a really bad date. Most of her dates were nice, but not the fit she was looking for.

She had been single for eight years, but only started looking for a man four years ago. She was picky, and didn't want to make a mistake again by ending up with the wrong man. She would be fixed up or search the Internet dating sites for someone.

One night before she went to bed, she sat down at her computer and viewed her dating site. On this particular night, she had been contacted by seven men. Her rule was that whoever contacted her must have at least three pictures to look at, in which he was not wearing sunglasses, wearing a hat, or posing with his shirt off. She had learned the hard way about going out with a man who looked nothing like his photo because he was wearing a hat and sunglasses.

Out of the seven men she looked at, one struck her as a possibility. He was age appropriate, 5'10", with short, greyish hair. He wrote her that he would be interested in having a conversation if she found him interesting.

She wrote him back, asking him for his cell number. He must have been online at the same time, as within ten minutes she received a message with his cell number. He told her that he would be up for another few hours, and to call him if she was up for having a conversation.

She had no objection to calling him, so she dialed his number. The phone did not ring more than once before he answered in a rather deep voice. She thought it was extremely sexy. She laughed to herself, thinking that it sounded like she'd dialed one of those 900 numbers.

His name was Eddie, and he owned a shoe repair shop. It was a family business, and he was the third generation to own the shop. He had been single for 10 years and told her that he would like to eventually try marriage again. With the right person, of course. He had a daughter who was 27. She didn't have any children, but liked being with men who did.

They spoke for about 30 minutes and, before saying goodnight, agreed to go out the following Saturday night. They would meet at a mutually agreed-upon spot, and then he would drive to a restaurant for dinner.

After hanging up, she felt a touch of excitement. Maybe, just maybe, this would work out. She knew that she was very optimistic about new men, but repeatedly disappointed. She was a very positive person and gave people the benefit of the doubt all the time. It was Tuesday, and in four days she would be elated or disappointed.

She wanted to look really good so, on the day of her date, she had a manicure and pedicure and a trim of her long, brunette hair. She was feeling good about herself. It would take her fifteen minutes to get to the meeting place, so she left her house at 7:15 pm for the 7:30 meeting.

She was right on time. She parked her Lexus and waited in the car. She told him what she was driving and vice versa, so she was looking for Jeep wagon.

At 7:35, she saw the Jeep pull into the parking lot and stop right next to her. The Jeep must have been 15 years old, and the body needed lots of work. It actually looked like it had been in a demolition derby and lost.

She felt like telling him that she would drive, but thought against it. He resembled his pictures, but she knew that the pictures must have been a few years old. Maybe not as old as the Jeep, but within a few years.

They both got out of their cars and shook hands before he opened his car door for her to get in. She made sure she looked at the seat, as she did not want a spring to stick her in the ass.

The Jeep had a musty odor. Actually, Eddie smelled the same way. Her intuition told her to just leave, but she couldn't bring herself to do such a thing. She tried to control her gag reflex. He had on a nice shirt, but his pants needed to be pressed; she couldn't begin to count the wrinkles.

Eddie told her that he made reservations at a restaurant about half an hour away. She immediately looked to see if there were any vomit bags in the car, like the ones airplanes have. At times, she felt that being too nice a person was not so good.

They were about halfway there when the engine light lit up. She noticed smoke coming from under the hood. She couldn't believe what was about to happen.

Eddie pulled the Jeep to the side of the road, and got out to open the hood. When he did, smoke poured out of the engine. He became very upset and started a barrage of bad language. He paid no attention to Iris, and actually forgot that she was there. He was beside himself.

He pulled out his cell phone and called for a tow truck. Without apologizing or saying anything, he began pacing along the dark road while Iris just sat in the Jeep with the windows open. She had no idea what to say to console him. She knew one thing for sure — this was a one-and-done date.

All this time, he didn't speak to her. The tow truck arrived and, after a brief conversation with the driver, he finally said something to Iris. What he said was just plain unbelievable.

He told her that she would have to take a cab back to her car, and didn't even offer her cabfare. Then he walked back and watched as the tow truck driver hoisted the old beater of a Jeep to tow it somewhere.

Iris watched as he got into the truck with the driver and pulled away, just leaving her to stand on the street and wait for a cab. She had to walk a few blocks to figure out where she was, so she could tell the cab where to pick her up.

When she got home, she was really pissed off and had to get the last word in. She emailed Eddie and told him what she thought of him, that he should take that smelly old Jeep of his to the place where they crush cars, and that he should get in the front seat before they crushed it.

Unbelievable!

FACEBOOK

Roger had been divorced from his second wife for a little more than three years. He was good looking and knew it, and he took pride in dating nice-looking ladies. His two ex-wives were very attractive women. Being six-foot-three with a good, slender build, he had no problem getting dates.

He did not believe that he would ever go on any dating sites because of all the stories he heard from his friends. He would never get caught going out with a woman who he had never laid eyes on before.

He was a big man on campus during his school days, a good athlete with many, many friends. All the girls wanted to go out with him, and he had his pick of the litter.

He had more than twelve hundred friends and acquaintances on Facebook, and would go on Facebook every night. This was one way of keeping in touch with friends he had all over the country. Every day, someone would try to friend him. Some he knew, and some he did not.

One night while looking at the people who wanted to friend him, he saw a woman he recognized. First the name Ruby, and then her headshot. His memory brought him back to his high school days. He had always wanted to go out with Ruby but, at that time, she was dating a man she eventually married.

They knew each other in school, but were never really close. As he remembered, Ruby was absolutely stunning. She was tall, with a great figure and long, blonde hair. She was a year behind him and was dating a college guy then. Roger didn't know much about her, only that she had all the boys drooling wanting to go out with her.

So, here she was on Facebook asking to be his friend. He was curious, and accepted her friending. He had not laid eyes on her in 30 years. He wondered, did she still look as beautiful 30 years later? Was she still married? Did she have any children?

He typed her a message telling her that he was happy she'd friended him. He also asked her for her number and sent her his.

Looking at her Facebook page, he saw that she was now single and living about 30 minutes away from him. She had also posted pictures of her daughters and two grandchildren. Her daughters were quite good looking.

He looked at more than 30 of her pictures, but didn't find any of Ruby except for her headshot in which, after 30 years, she still looked great. He was very anxious to speak to her.

He picked up his cell phone and dialed her number. They talked about their days in school and played the name game. After about 15 minutes of playing "Do you remember this?" they started talking about the last 30 years.

She told him she was divorced after 20 years of marriage, because she caught her husband sleeping with one of her friends. She worshipped her grandchildren and lived a simple life. She did not date, as she had no interest in it.

Roger told her all about his past, which seemed to be more exciting than hers. He was very successful in everything, except for his personal life. Two failed marriages were nothing to be proud of.

He told her that he'd had a terrible crush on her in school and wanted to go out with her. In his mind, he remembered this beauty who had all the great physical qualities any man would want.

He told her that he would not take no for an answer. She was reluctant, but finally gave in. He had to wait 30 years to go out with his former crush, but it was finally going to happen.

He made reservations at an upscale restaurant. He asked for outside seating, seeing that the weather was quite nice. He wanted this date to be great. This was the one girl he always wanted but could never get.

He'd found out that Ruby lived in a lower economic area, in a condo on the 15th floor. He'd visualized her living in a large home with all the amenities.

He parked his car and headed for her building's entrance. It took about four minutes for the elevator to arrive. His anticipation was growing, and for him that was quite unusual. He'd never been like this before. He couldn't wait for this beautiful lady to open the door.

The elevator finally made it up to her floor. As he took a walk down the hall, he checked to see that his shirt was tucked in and his zipper was up. He wanted to make an immediate good impression as soon as she opened the door.

He took a deep breath and knocked. When the door opened, he was in complete shock. There she was, with a rather nice-looking face but a body that was ... big. She must've weighed 300 pounds. He couldn't believe what he was seeing.

He wished that he could just turn around and walk out the door, but didn't want to hurt her feelings. Now he knew why there were no pictures of her on Facebook.

It was quite comical watching her get into his little sports car. He didn't know how she'd get back out of it. If this had been a fix-up, he would've thought someone was playing a joke on him.

He knew that she must know many of the same people he did, and he didn't want her to speak ill of him. So, he took her to dinner and talked about many things, but never said that he wanted to see her again.

Roger learned a valuable lesson about going out with someone he hadn't seen in years without seeing a current photograph. One thing was for sure; she couldn't say anything bad about him, as he was a gentleman throughout the entire evening.

When he walked her to her condo, he gave her a hug. If she'd hugged him back, he might've dislocated a rib.

Live and learn.

NEVER SATISFIED

Marshall had always been a ladies' man. He never married, and never came close; he liked his single lifestyle. He knew he was a good-looking man who took care of himself by watching his diet and working out five days a week.

He was 48 and looked several years younger. He thanked his parents for the good genes. He had a full head of hair and always seemed to have a tan.

His job as an accountant kept him very busy — too busy to go out in the evenings and search for his next relationship. With that said, he chose to seek a woman online. This he could do every night without leaving his home. Marshall would receive about 10 emails per week from women who were also seeking a relationship. They all said they loved his pictures and his profile.

Like most men, he was selective in who he responded to. He had his rules, such as no smokers, no one older than he was, and no women taller than his 5'10" height.

He was sure that women had their parameters, too. He was quite critical, and maybe a little too judgmental. But that was him, and he couldn't — or wouldn't — change.

One night while he was looking at his emails, a woman got his attention. She was the right age, 45, and attractive. As he read her profile, he saw that she had never been married, just like himself. She was 5'5" and appeared to be in great shape.

She wrote him a short note and included her cell number. She wrote that she was interested in speaking and not emailing. That was perfectly fine with him. He wasted no time and dialed her number. He didn't know her name, as she just signed her email "BK."

She picked up the phone when he called, and within 20 seconds he found out her name was Bunny. He had to ask the question immediately, as he needed to know what to call her.

They had a decent conversation and talked about the usual things like family, where they grew up, and where they went to school. All the preliminaries for a first conversation.

He found out that she owned a very high-end woman's boutique. She sounded a little stuck up, but he could deal with that. He had been out with many women over the years, and felt he could handle or adjust to anybody.

Marshall asked her about her availability to get together, as he knew the retail business had grueling hours. He was a little more flexible than she was in terms of his hours.

So, they both looked at their schedules and decided to meet the following week at seven, at a restaurant near her shop. He figured they would have a drink and see if they wanted to see each other again. He had been burned a few times by meeting someone for dinner on the first date. It was not going to happen again. If they liked each other, then dinner was a possibility.

He arrived at 6:45 and grabbed a stool at the bar. He knew that this place would be expensive just by the ambiance. He was right, as he ordered a drink that cost $13 — and that was before the tip.

At 7:05, Bunny walked in. At first sight, he thought she looked better in her pictures. She recognized him and grabbed the stool right next to his. She ordered a bloody mary, which might have cost $15 looking at the size of it.

They talked for about an hour, or two drinks each. He was right in his assessment that she was stuck up. She must have used forty-five minutes talking about herself. Down deep, he knew why she was never married. Any normal man would've strangled her. He figured that, being in the retail business, she had to talk, and she was good at it. He had to laugh to himself, thinking that she probably brushed her teeth with Ben-Gay to get her jaws ready for the next day.

It was 8:15 and he thought he'd had enough when she blurted out, "Let's have dinner." It caught him by complete surprise. Before he could muster a sound, she got up and headed for the hostess to get a table.

He figured that he was hungry and another hour wouldn't kill him. He paid the bar tab, which was $88. It wasn't that he couldn't afford it, but she never offered to chip in.

When he viewed the menu, he almost had an accident in his pants. The cheapest salad was $24 and a chop steak was $32. He started to feel like she was taking advantage of him. She ordered a salad with salmon for $32, and another cocktail. He ordered the broiled chicken, which was $27. Everything was a la cart. So the potato and salad he ordered weren't included with the price of his entree. He hoped that the meal would arrive soon, as he didn't want to pay for another one of those expensive drinks.

The meal came, and his chicken looked good. For $27, this chicken breast should start singing. Her meal looked good but, after tasting the salmon, she asked the waiter to take it back, saying it tasted funny.

The waiter took it back and said he would get her a fresh one. Meanwhile, she ordered another drink while waiting for her new salad.

She was starting to slur her words. Who wouldn't after five or six drinks? Finally, her new salad arrived. After tasting the salmon, she was still dissatisfied. Maybe it was the alcohol that caused her to act this way. The waiter was kind enough to ask her if she would like something different. Marshall started to worry that she would ask for a steak, and hoped that she would order nothing so he could get away from her and go home. If he had been a schmuck, he would've left already.

Wouldn't you know it? She ordered a strip steak for $40. He was almost finished with his meal when her steak arrived. If she'd sent that back, he would've gone to the restroom and not returned. He thought about it anyway.

She took about three or four bites from the steak and said she didn't want any more. She asked for a box so she could take it home. By now, she was quite wasted.

When the check arrived, all $110 of it, she got up from the table, thanked him for dinner, and told him she didn't think they were a good match. She then turned and left the restaurant. He'd spent $200 and proceeded to cuss the whole ride home.

After this, Marshall figured that he would change the way he did things. From now on, he would meet a woman at a coffee shop. If she wanted to eat, he would proudly buy her a donut.

THE OUTHOUSE

James had had many different dating experiences in the eight years since his divorce. He had some wonderful dates and some terrible ones, but he was the kind of person who would never give up trying to find that right woman.

He was fixed up, he met women at the grocery store, and he was on every dating site. Finding dates was no problem for him. Finding that elusive "perfect" woman was what he and every other single man was trying to do.

Each time he would go on a first date, he would get excited, thinking it might be the date where he met his dream girl. Being a nice-looking man in his 50s, James thought he would have no trouble finding her.

He must have gone out with hundreds of girls in his eight years of dating. Sometimes, he thought something must be wrong with him. Maybe he was too particular in what he was looking for.

He was on the computer one Friday afternoon, searching one of his dating sites. One woman stuck out as being attractive and age-appropriate at 52. Of course, he had met many women who weren't honest about their ages. He never minded if someone fudged their age by a couple of years, but some women more than fudged. Some said they were 10 to 15 years younger.

James decided to drop this attractive woman an email to see if she was interested in talking. If he wrote 10 women a week, maybe two or three would answer back. He could never figure out why a woman didn't answer a good-looking guy with a good profile.

He figured that if he received no reply in a few days, then she wasn't interested. He had a rule that if a woman didn't answer him, he would not try to contact her again.

Well, lo and behold, he received an answer from her. She wrote a rather long email and said she would be happy to get a call from him. She wrote her phone number and signed the email with her name, Anna.

James waited until he got home from his office to call her. It was around six when he put the key in the door, and he needed an hour to unwind before calling. He poured a glass of wine and sat in his easy chair, getting himself psyched up to call.

He dialed her number, and Anna picked up after three rings. Her voice was rather deep, but he was making no judgements about that, or anything else for that matter. Anna was an events planner, which took up quite a bit of her time. She was divorced twice and had one son, who was away at college.

They spoke for about 20 minutes and decided to go to the state fair the next Saturday, as she had some business to take care of there. A decision was made that they would meet at a place where she could park her car, and he would drive them.

He was always early, no matter where he went. He had time to wash his car and clean the inside. She showed up right on time. He took a look at her when she got out of her car. If she was 52, he would go streaking at the fair. She must have fudged her age by at least eight years. She had long hair in her photo, but now it was extremely short. Her figure was shaped like a pear. If he'd had the guts, he would've driven off, but he wasn't that kind of guy.

She got into the car, and off they went. He couldn't say too much as she was a real talker, what he would call a motor mouth. This was going to be a long afternoon. At least they were going to a place that he wanted to go. Maybe her business would keep her occupied and he could be on his own.

Her business took about 30 minutes, which was far from enough time for him to walk around without her. He was a complete gentleman and offered to buy lunch, which she took him up on. She could eat, as she had a plate of fried chicken, mashed potatoes, and two ears of corn. She washed it down with a beer.

It was almost five, time for them to leave and head back. On their way to the car, he started to smell something that was not too appetizing. He didn't want to embarrass her, so he just tried to ignore the terrible odor. With everything she ate, he wondered why she hadn't exploded.

Before they got to the car, she mentioned that she had to use the Porta-Potty before they left. Boy, was he glad, as he didn't have a bedpan in his car. He watched as she opened the door to the Porta-Potty and went in. He hated those things, especially after a long day of hundreds of people using them.

He looked at his watch, and she had been in there for at least 10 minutes. Maybe she did explode. After about 10 more minutes, he heard a banging on the door from the inside. When he got closer, he heard her yelling. He didn't even want to know what was happening, but he just couldn't avoid it.

James stood next to the door and asked her what was wrong. She told him that she couldn't open the door, as the latch was stuck. He tried to open it from the outside, but his efforts were futile. He had no choice but to try and get help.

He asked several men to help him. They tried yanking and pulling, with no luck. One time, they almost knocked it over on its side. If that happened, James would be driving home alone.

Finally someone used a crowbar, which opened the door. She was so embarrassed that her face turned beet red. She was in there so long that her clothes didn't smell too good.

Needless to say, the ride home seemed like it took hours. James had a hard time with the odor in the car. He knew he would have to fumigate it as soon as possible. The funny part about the way the date ended was, before getting out of the car, she told him she thought he was a very nice man but she didn't think they were a good match.

He almost burst out laughing when she told him that. He never uttered a word, and just drove off. He couldn't wait to tell his friends this story. He was thinking that if the outhouse had tipped over, he would've needed a paramedic —for himself, because he would've lost consciousness from laughing so hard.

THAT DARN BACK POCKET

Mimi was probably one of the nicest ladies a man could meet. She would always give a man a chance. She just had to have honesty, and didn't like it when anyone told her a lie.

Divorced for seven years, with a 20-year-old son, she wanted to find that elusive final date and get herself out of the horrible singles scene. She was on several dating sites and had around three dates per month.

She was not bad looking, and had a decent body thanks to yoga classes. She would take a morning class and then head to the jewelry store that she owned. She had her own money and didn't need a man to support he. She brought enough to the table all by herself.

She had plenty of dates, with most of them being one-and-dones. Like all other single people, she had her preferences, but was willing to give every man she went out with a chance.

One evening while searching the dating sites, she saw that she had a message from a man who said he was interested in her, as he liked her looks and profile.

She immediately looked at his profile. What she saw was a decent-looking man of about 55, who appeared to be in somewhat decent shape. His profile said he was a few pounds overweight, which didn't bother her.

She decided to write him back and give him her cell number. She asked him to call her any evening after nine, as she would definitely be home by then.

The next night her phone rang, and it was Herman. He told her to call him Herm. He told her that he worked at a restaurant in a big hotel. He'd been single for 10 years and had no children.

Herm sounded decent enough for her to accept a date to meet him. He asked her out to dinner without even meeting first. For some reason, she said she would meet him for dinner. It had been quite some time since she met someone for dinner without meeting for a cup of coffee or a drink first.

They agreed to meet at a Mexican restaurant on a Wednesday night at eight. She would go there straight from work, as the restaurant they chose was equidistant from where each of them worked.

She arrived at 7:45 and took a seat in the bar area. She told him that she would be wearing a red dress that he couldn't miss. She ordered a margarita while she waited.

Around 8:05, a man walked in who didn't resemble the photo she saw on her computer. He was older than his picture by maybe seven to 10 years. His profile said he was a few pounds overweight, but he must have meant *many* pounds. His belt was pulled up almost to his chest and his behind was so huge you could show a movie on it. She had been lied to, but she was hungry. She just wanted to eat and then say good-night.

Not once during the evening did she mention his dishonesty. What would she gain by doing that, anyway? She ordered a burrito dinner, and couldn't wait for it to arrive. He ordered a taco platter, which came with rice and beans.

When he finished, they could've put the plate back on the shelf without washing it; it didn't have a speck on it. Their conversation was mainly about work and the upcoming election. She saw no need to tell him about her private life, as she would never see him again.

When the waiter brought the check, she offered to split it. Herm refused which was a gentlemanly thing to do. He appeared to go into the back pocket of his slacks to get his wallet. She saw him struggling to get it out. He started to break out in a sweat as the struggle continued. Finally, she offered to help him get his wallet out. When he got up, she noticed that the pocket was so narrow and his wallet was so thick that she didn't know how he got it in there in the first place.

She eventually gave up, but he continued to struggle. The sweat was running down his face, and at one point she heard something that she knew was a fart. She ignored it, not wanting to embarrass him any further.

Finally, she'd had enough. She pulled out her credit card and gave it to the waiter. When the waiter came back, she signed the slip, said good-night, and told Herm that he should be more honest with women. Then she disappeared out the door.

On her drive home, she started thinking that she should never, ever go out with someone without meeting them first.

ARE YOU FOR REAL?

Hal was an extremely eligible bachelor, and he knew it. He was good-looking, 30 years old, and the owner of his own insurance agency. He had no trouble finding women to go out with, but he wanted to find the right girl, settle down, and start a family.

He had dated all kinds of women, mostly from the Internet. He would occasionally go out with older women, but he preferred someone between 24 and 30. Finding the right girl is hard, no matter how old a person is. He heard all the stories from his friends about women who were not honest. He was sure men were the same, fudging their ages and descriptions.

One evening while surfing dating sites, he noticed an attractive women who fit right into his age bracket. Her smile just froze him, and he knew he must contact her. He always got his hopes up, which he knew was a mistake. He was disappointed more often than not.

He wrote her a long email, telling her that he was very interested in talking to her, and left his cell number. He was hoping that she would call. The ball was in her court.

After three days, he had a voicemail on his phone. Her name was Robyn, and her voice was soft and sweet. Hal couldn't wait to get home from the office so he could call her.

It was around seven when he decided to call. He took a deep breath and dialed her number on his cell phone. The phone rang three times before she picked up. When she said hello, he melted, as her voice was so young and tender.

Their conversation lasted 30 minutes. In that time, he found out that she lived about 30 minutes away, was married for a very short time at age 20, and was a receptionist at a doctor's office. She sounded eager to meet him. Before hanging up, they agreed to meet the following week for dinner.

Hal usually didn't take someone to dinner on the first date, but he would make an exception for Robyn. That face and voice were all he could think about for hours upon hours. His hopes were sky-high.

On the way to pick her up at her home, he stopped to pick up a dozen red roses and a box of chocolates. He wanted to make a great impression. He'd never done this before.

He was about 10 minutes away, and he was starting to feel nervous, which was uncharacteristic for him. He didn't want to show how he felt. He wanted to come across as a confident man who was a complete gentleman.

He pulled into the complex and drove around until he saw the address on her unit. He parked the car and took out the flowers and candy. He took a deep breath and headed for her door.

He rang the bell and waited with anticipation for the door to open. When it did, he froze in his tracks. She had the most beautiful face and gorgeous, long, brunette hair ... but she was about seven months pregnant!

He didn't know what to say. How could this happen to him? The only thing he could do was ask why she didn't mention her' situation" to him. She replied that, if she did, he wouldn't want to meet her. She was 100 percent correct. about that!

Hal politely handed her the flowers and candy and said good-night, as he was still stunned. When would he ever learn not to get his hopes up? The higher they went, the further he fell when reality hit.

NOT IN THE SHRUBS

Janet had no problem finding men to go out with. The trouble was that most of them were one-and-dones. She knew she was picky. Why shouldn't she be? She was a good-looking, 38-year-old woman who was in excellent shape and had a decent job managing a dental office. She'd been married briefly 10 years earlier, and would marry again when the right partner came along.

She felt she should give men more of a chance than she had been giving them. She was too quick to judge, and knew that was wrong. So, she made a pact with herself to be more tolerant, get to know her dates, and not make such quick decisions.

She looked at the Internet every night before she went to bed. At least five men wrote her every day. On this particular night, she received a message from a very nice-looking man of about 40. He wrote and told her that he thought she was beautiful, and that they had many things in common. He left his number and asked her to call him if she was interested.

Janet usually didn't make the first move, but she had a different feeling in this case. She would give him a call and, if she didn't like the conversation, she would just use her favorite term. Next!

So, she called him and he picked up on the second ring. His name was Lucas, and she liked the way he sounded. They spoke about the usual things that two people talk about during their first conversation.

They talked for about an hour, which was a long time for a first conversation. At the very end of their talk, he told her that he was in between jobs. She would normally consider that a red flag, but the new Janet was going to give him a chance. Times were hard and many people had lost their jobs, so she couldn't hold that against him.

He suggested that they go hit golf balls and then go to dinner. She thought that it would be fun. She was wondering how he knew she was a golfer, but then realized it was listed in her profile under things she liked to do. At least he read her profile, unlike some others.

The date was set for a Sunday. They didn't live far from each other, but she wanted to meet him at the golf range and then drive together to the restaurant.

That morning, he called to tell her that his truck wouldn't start and asked if she could pick him up. She really didn't want to, but said she would. He gave her directions, which led her to a really dumpy area. It was so dumpy that she wouldn't have been surprised if she saw a *Sanford and Son* truck parked nearby.

She pulled up to his building and waited for him to come out. She waited five minutes before he came out, bringing his driver with him. He looked like his photo, maybe even a little better. He jumped in the car, and off they went to the driving range they went.

They hit golf balls for 45 minutes, and he had at least four beers in that time. She wondered how a man without a job could afford to spend money like that, but she didn't know his financial situation. Maybe he had money saved, or had inherited some. It really wasn't any of her business.

It was a good thing he wasn't driving. If she'd had four beers in that short period of time, she would be on the floor. She couldn't drink beer, as it made her sick. She did like her wine, though.

When she drove to dinner, he directed her to a nice restaurant on a hill, with a nice patio overlooking a golf course. She parked her car. As soon as they got out, he took her hand and led her up through a flowerbed and onto the patio. The sidewalk would've been better, as people stared at them on their upward journey.

They grabbed a table and he ordered another beer, while she ordered a glass of wine. He asked her if she would have at least two glasses, which she said she would, so he ordered a bottle. He finished his beer and started drinking wine. She noticed he was starting to slur his words, and his eyes had bocame glassy.

When the waiter came by to take their food order, she ordered a salad with salmon. Lucas decided that he wasn't hungry and ordered nothing.

Janet was getting irritated and knew that this was another one-and-done. He was drunk. What happened next completely stunned her. He got up, excused himself, and disappeared into the bushes. *He was urinating in the bushes!* He came back at the same time that her salad arrived. Without asking, he put his unwashed hands in her salad and took a piece of her salmon.

That was the last straw. She went into her purse, took out $50, and put it on the table. She told him to get a cab home, and stormed off.

She was going back to her old ways, deciding that not everyone deserved a chance. She was thoroughly disgusted, and would take a few days off from her computer.

THE WOODEN LEG

Molly was a happy individual and everybody liked liked her. She was outgoing, with a five-star personality. She worked as a sales girl in a high-end women's clothing store, and had quite a following. She could sell ice in winter, as she made everyone feel comfortable.

Her life was good, but it lacked one thing. She wanted to meet someone she could connect with. She had been fixed up several times, but her luck was not good. She had been on dating sites on and off for more than two years. When she felt frustrated, she took a break.

She was a nice-looking woman who was in decent shape. She knew that men were visual, and always wanted to look her best at all times. She never knew who she would meet.

It was spring, and she was feeling the urge to go back online to see if anything had changed with the men on the site. It had been two months, maybe there was someone new.

It didn't take her long to see a man who appealed to her. His photo showed a good-looking man sitting in his car. He was tan and, if his photo was recent, he looked about 50 years old.

She knew how people tended to fudged their ages; she'd even lowered her age by three years. His profile said that he was divorced with two children. He lived about an hour away, and had some of the same interests she did.

Molly sent him a message asking him to read her profile. She said he should email her if he liked what he saw. She didn't expect to hear from him, as she usually got about two responses for every 10 messages sent.

Three days later, she received a message telling her that he was interested in having a conversation. He left his cell number and asked her to call.

Thursday night, at about 8:30 when she got home from work, she poured herself a glass of wine and unwound for 30 minutes, before deciding to call.

His name was Ralph, and he picked up the phone on the second ring. The conversation was the same as most first conversations, just the basics and a little history about each other.

Before hanging up, they decided to meet at a bar in between where they lived, at a time convenient for both of them.

The bar was like the one on "Cheers," crowded and apparently full of regulars. Molly arrived first. She found two barstools, plopped herself down on one, and waited. She ordered a Grey Goose and cranberry juice, and watched the door for Ralph's arrival.

She didn't have to wait long. When he came in, she almost fell off the barstool. He had a peg leg! Not an artificial leg that resembled a real one, but a peg leg like Long John Silver.

She would've liked to know this beforehand, and felt it was important enough for him to tell her about during their conversation. This shook her up, and put a damper on their meeting.

She didn't want to be shallow, but this wouldn't work for her. She asked him what happened, and he told her that he lost his leg in a motorcycle accident.

They talked for an hour and then she excused herself, telling him that she had to open the shop the next morning. She said good-night and left.

This was a real first for her. She was sure that some girls wouldn't object, but not being told beforehand really was a deal-breaker.

BODY ODOR

Paula will never go out with a fix-up again. She must've been fixed up at least 10 times, and each one was worse than the last. She had such a hard time meeting men that her friends were always trying to fix her up.

She was divorced for five years after a rather rocky marriage. She couldn't believe that she'd been married for only seven years. Things went bad after the first year, as the honeymoon was over.

At least she had no children and no baggage. She had a decent job as a dental hygienist, which paid her well. She wanted to look into a man's eyes instead of his open mouth.

One day, the receptionist at her office told her about a friend of the man she was dating. Of course, Paula was all ears. She had the feeling, as she did with other fix-ups, that maybe this one would work.

She told her friend that she was interested, and gave permission to give out her number. She knew that she shouldn't get her hopes up, but she couldn't help herself.

It didn't take long before Harold called her. She told him that she was expecting his call and was looking forward to hearing from him.

Harold had never been married, and also had no baggage. He seemed to have lots of things in common with her. He liked movies and photography, which she also really liked.

They talked for more than an hour and decided to go out. Paula came up with the idea that maybe they should do a double date with her receptionist friend and her boyfriend. Harold thought that was a good idea. He said he would call his friend and ask him if they could double the following Friday night.

Everything was set. She would be picked up at seven, and the four of them would go to dinner. She liked this idea, as the first date was usually the hardest one. This way, it was not one-on-one, and there was no pressure.

She waited downstairs at her apartment for them to pick her up. She didn't even know what Harold looked like. All she knew about him was what she heard in their initial phone conversation.

A car pulled up at 7:05, and she saw her friend in the passenger seat. At first she didn't notice Harold in the backseat. When they stopped, the back door opened, and out rolled Harold.

Vintage Robert Redford he was not. He was about 5'9" and about 50 pounds overweight. He had a scruffy beard, and she couldn't tell if he'd forgotten to shave or was trying to grow a beard. His hair was kind of messy, and he was dressed like he was going to a bar with his friends. Bad first impression made.

She couldn't turn back now. She got in the car and braced herself for a long evening. At least there was another couple with them. She didn't know what she would've done if it was alone with him.

On the ride to the restaurant, she noticed a musty smell. It seemed to get worse as the night progressed. She wasn't quite sure if it was Harold or if they'd runover a skunk.

The restaurant was nice, and it even had music. They had a table in the lounge area. Each ordered a drink, and they talked about politics and sports. Two favorite topics for the men.

When the band played a slow song, Paula's friend and her boyfriend hit the dance floor. Paula was praying that Harold did not know how to dance.

Wrong! He asked her to dance. How could she say no? As soon as they got close, the musty smell mystery was solved. It was coming from Harold. She wanted to throw up as he held her tight. Why hadn't anyone told him about this horrid smell? Maybe they didn't want to embarrass him.

The two hours at the restaurant felt like 12. After dinner, Harold suggested a place that he knew for some after-dinner drinks. Paula was thinking it was probably a biker bar where no one ever took a bath. He would feel right at home.

Paula then said she was not feeling well and asked if they could drive her home. Another 30 minutes and she would've lost her dinner.

Once she got home, she was in the shower in a flash. Thank goodness he didn't try to kiss her goodnight. She would've passed out.

On Monday at the office, she asked her friend if she smelled anything in the car. Her friend admitted had smelled something foul, but didn't have the heart to say anything.

Paula thanked her for trying. It must have taken a week to get that odor out of her nose. This date was not just bad; it stunk!

BUSTED

Ande had a hard time meeting someone. She didn't want to put herself on the Internet, as she'd heard too many horror stories. She would take her chances by having her friends fix her up.

Unfortunately, her friends didn't know many men to fix her up with. She was a nice-looking lady of 49 who was a receptionist for a cable company. Her job didn't give her the luxury of meeting men.

She'd been married once for 10 years, and had a 24-year-old daughter who lived on the West Coast. She always hoped that she would meet someone on her many visits out west, but each time she came home disappointed.

Many times, she just wanted to give up, believing that she would never have another man in her life. She felt that maybe it was her destiny.

One day after work, she decided to go to Whole Foods and pick up something for dinner. The salad bar was crowded, so she just stood there, waiting her turn. She was standing in back of a man. She couldn't tell what he looked like from the front, but he was tall, about 6'4". She was 5'10", so she thought that was ideal for her.

Unexpectedly, he turned around and started a conversation with her. He was good looking, and she hoped that she looked good after a long day at work.

He introduced himself as Paul. He was a financial adviser and was also picking up some dinner. They made small talk and he asked her to go in front of him in the line. He was a gentleman, and they seemed to hit it off.

After they made their salads, they decided to grab some coffee and continue their conversation. Ande couldn't believe this was happening to her. Meeting a man at the salad bar! She secretly wanted him to ask for her phone number.

He did better than that. He asked her to go with him to a baseball game, as he was a season-ticket holder with great seats. She didn't care for baseball, but quickly said yes. She would've said yes to watching grasshoppers jump if he'd asked her.

The seats were great. Sitting in the first row makes it hard not to enjoy anything, except for a play where you would have to look up to watch the performance.

Ande was having a great time. She had a few beers and a hotdog, and was enjoying talking to Paul more than watching the ballgame. At the seventh-inning stretch, she got up and sang with everyone else.

Even though it was a weeknight and she had to get up for work the next day, she didn't care, as she was having a really good time. She hadn't enjoyed herself like this for a long time. Paul even held her hand during the game. She knew that he liked her just by his actions. The feeling was mutual, and she didn't want the night to end.

Around eleven o'clock, he drove her home. Even though it was late, she asked if he would like to come inside. He looked at his watch as he stepped inside. Not many men had been inside her home. She had a nice place, decorated very modern, which he noticed.

They talked for about 15 minutes, and then he made the bold move to kiss her. She didn't resist, and they started to make out. Or, as some people say, kick it.

The simple kiss turned into a very heated session. She hadn't been with a man in a very long time. She was feeling like a born-again virgin.

They had sex on the couch and never made it upstairs. This wasn't like her, but she couldn't help herself. She would do it again and again, with no regrets.

Before he left, he took her phone number and said he would call her. She felt the ball was in his court, and she could only hope he would call.

She didn't have to wait very long. The next day, he called to say hello. They talked for a few minutes, then he told her that he had a customer and would call her later. She wrote down the number from her caller ID, and decided she would call him if he didn't call her by the end of the day.

At 4:55, she dialed his number, hoping he would pick up the phone. Instead, she got an operator who told her that Paul was gone for the day. She asked the operator where the bank was located.

She had a plan. She was going to take a half day off and surprise him by taking him to lunch. How could he not appreciate that offer?

The next day, she worked until 11:30, then got in her car and drove to his bank. She wanted to see the look of surprise on his face. She parked the car and walked in. She went up to the lady in the information booth and asked where she could find Paul.

The answer she got nearly floored her. She was told that Paul and his wife just left for lunch. *His wife!*

She didn't know if she should scream or yell. She was devastated. How could she let him get away with doing something like that to her? She had to do something.

She decided to wait for Paul and his wife to come back from lunch. She was hoping that his wife would walk back into the bank, but she positioned herself so that even if the wife didn't come in, she would hopefully see them outside.

She was in luck. She noticed Paul and his wife walking toward the bank. She knew exactly what she was going to say. She wanted him to wet his pants when he saw her.

Ande did not wait for them to walk in. She went outside to intercept them. Paul's mouth almost hit the floor when he saw her. He didn't have much time to react.

Ande kissed him on the cheek while his wife watched in disbelief. Ande then asked if this was his wife, though she already knew the answer. The women said she was, and asked who Ande was. Ande calmly told her that she'd gone to a ballgame with Paul the night before, and that they'd slept together afterward.

With that said, Ande turned around and walked away, leaving Paul to deal with his pissed-off wife. She felt good about doing what she did. She didn't know she had it in her but, after how he'd hurt her, it was total justice.

THE TRUNK

When Gail was asked if she ever had a date that always stuck in her mind, she would always tell the same story about a date she had many years ago.

She was fixed up with a man named Oscar. A mutual friend thought they would be a good match. They spoke on the phone several times before they met, which she preferred.

They seemed to hit it off on the phone as they got to know about each other. They had much in common. He liked sports and movies, and so did she. They compared movies that they thought were good, and didn't disagree on many. She liked basketball, football, and tennis; he liked basketball, football, baseball, and hockey.

Since they seemed to know each other, they both felt comfortable about their first meeting. He suggested a movie and then getting something to eat. She thought that would be a nice first date.

He asked her if she would like to see a double feature at the drive-in. She hadn't been to a drive-in for a long time, and thought it would be different and fun. The date was set for the following Saturday night.

She felt comfortable with him picking her up. Usually she didn't allow a man to pick her up until she was really comfortable, no matter how many dates it took. In this case, though, they were set up by a mutual friend.

She was excited to see the movies. Normally it would be a mistake to see a movie on a first date, but in this case it was all right. They'd had enough phone time and knew the basic information about each other before the date.

Oscar drove a large Buick. It was like a boat. He was nice-looking, and she was pleased. She hoped that he liked the way she looked, too.

The drive-in was 15 minutes from her home, but with traffic the ride was longer. They had plenty of time to get there before the first movie started.

Just before they got there, he pulled over and, in a serious way, asked her a question that she would never forget. He asked her if she could get in the trunk so he would only have to pay for one person. He said that way he would have a few dollars leftover to get something to eat.

She didn't know if he was kidding. She asked him to repeat the question, which he did without flinching. There was no way she was getting in his trunk. She couldn't believe what she was hearing.

She looked him straight in the eye and said she wouldn't be getting in the trunk, and that she could go without eating.

Needless to say, the evening changed for her. She had liked him — until he asked her that question.

After the movie, she asked him to take her home. She had no intention of seeing him again. She'd heard of cheap, but this took the cake.

THE DOG

Marci thought she'd finally met the man of her dreams on the Internet. He was handsome and tall, with a great build. He was age-appropriate, had been married before, and had two children.

She saw that he posted several photos, and he looked the same in all of them. She wasn't going to be fooled this time around.

She sent him a message, telling him she would like to know more about him. This was bold for her, as she rarely made the first move. She figured that she had nothing to lose. If he wrote back, that would be great. If he didn't reply, then she'd continue on her mission. About a week later, she got a response.

His name was Barry, and he'd been out of town, but noticed her message when he returned. He sent her a reply that said he would be interested in talking to her, and left his cell number.

She was excited, and wasted no time calling him. She figured there was no reason to wait. So, she poured herself a glass of wine, made herself comfortable on her new, plush white couch, and dialed him up.

The conversation went well. They had many things in common, and both wanted to meet as soon as possible.

Two days later, they met at Starbucks and seemed to hit it off. Barry was a big guy. He was 6'5" and must have been a weightlifter. Marci referred to him as Paul Bunyan. She was 5'3", and had to look up to him.

The meeting lasted about an hour, and both decided they would like to see each other again. She left feeling pretty good, and thought he had potential.

The plans were that he would pick her up and they would go out to dinner. She didn't want to go to a movie, as they wouldn't be able to talk.

Saturday night at about seven, her doorbell rang. He was right on time, which was a plus. She hated when people weren't punctual.

When she opened the door, she couldn't believe what she saw. There was this really big man, holding a really small dog. At first she didn't know if it was a real dog. This sight caught her completely by surprise. She couldn't wait for his explanation.

Barry told her that his dog, Bullet, was not well and had a problem with his anal gland. He didn't want to leave him at home, so he'd leave him in the car while they were at dinner.

He put the dog down and, within minutes, he was rubbing his ass on her beautiful white carpet. Then, Bullet jumped on her new white couch and started rubbing his ass on it, too.

She couldn't believe what she was seeing. First Paul Bunyan picks her up carrying a dog that could fit in her pocket. Then the dog with an anal gland problem rubs his ass on her carpet and new couch.

She looked at Barry and told him it was not going to work, and that it would be best if he left. She didn't want to hear anything from him, except "good-night!"

SEASICK

Gail was a happy-go-lucky lady of 45, who had many friends. She'd been married for a few years, but most them were not happy ones, so she pulled the plug and moved on. She didn't want to go on the dating sites that many people suggested to her. Her friends were always trying to fix her up.

On the July 4, a friend asked if she'd like to be fixed up with a friend of the man she was dating. Her friend went on to tell her that the man had a boat, and they planned on going out on the water on the 4th to party and watch the fireworks from the boat.

Gail agreed, mainly because she wasn't going to be alone with him. Normally, she wouldn't mind, but she wouldn't want to be alone on a boat on a first date.

The plan was that her friend and her boyfriend would pick Gail up, and then they would pick up a few bottles of wine and vodka. The food was already on the boat, so they didn't have to stop at the grocery store.

It was a warm day, with the temperature heading toward 95 degrees. She hoped it would be cooler on the water, and after the sun went down.

As they were driving to the marina, Gail's friend pointed out the boat to her. It was a pretty big sailboat. Gail was actually getting excited, as seeing the fireworks from the water was something she'd never done before. She'd heard from others that it was a splendid and magnificent way to view them.

As they boarded the boat, she was introduced to Mel, her date and the boat's owner. He seemed nice and cordial. He wasn't that attractive, and was a little heavier than what she was used to going out with. But that day she just wanted to have a good time.

Also on the boat was a little dog that would not stop barking until Mel picked it up. Gail wasn't really fond of dogs. But, what choice did she have? As long as the dog didn't jump up on her, she could tolerate it.

Mel pulled the boat out late in the afternoon. It was hot and Gail did something she hadn't done in years. She had a few beers, as she was really thirsty. The mistake she made was that she'd only had a bagel and coffee to eat all day.

Mel didn't pay much attention to her, as he was too involved with handling the boat. She was fine with that because she was feeling a little tipsy. She starting eating chips and salsa and cheese and crackers, hoping that putting something in her stomach would help.

Eventually, Mel dropped anchor and joined the party. He opened a bottle of wine and poured four glasses. Gail's legs felt like rubber by this point. The rocking boat was not doing her any favors, either. She was nauseous, a feeling that she hated.

She was getting seasick, besides being tipsy from the alcohol. She felt sick — and stuck. How could she tell everyone she wanted to go back to shore?

She was looking quite pale, and it was noticeable. Her friend mentioned that maybe they should head back to shore. Mel objected, saying he had no intention of going back now. In an hour, many more boats would be where they were, getting ready for the fireworks show.

Gail didn't want to puke, because she would've felt terribly embarrassed. Mel told her to go down to the cabin and lay down. She didn't hesitate, and slid open the door to the lower cabin.

Once down in the cabin, she was greeted by the little dog, who started yapping and yapping. She was sweating profusely and finally couldn't hold it anymore. She didn't get to the washroom in time, and threw up all over the floor. While she was puking, the dog kept yapping.

When Mel came to check on her and saw what had happened, he went ballistic. He was yelling that someone was going to have to clean the floor. The stench was pretty bad.

Instead of trying to help Gail, he went in the other direction. He was even yelling at her friend. He was being a complete jerk. Finally, he pulled up anchor and headed back to shore, all the while yelling that his Fourth of July was ruined and that he never wanted to be fixed up again. He was yapping as much as that obnoxious dog.

Once on solid ground, Gail started to feel better. She learned a lesson about drinking on an empty stomach and was not going on a sailboat again.

About six months later, Gail and her friend were at a bar with a bunch of friends. They were having a good time and laughing up a storm. There were about 17 people in their group, and everyone was telling funny stories.

When it was Gail's turn, she told about her experience being fixed up with a total jerk and his little yapping dog on the Fourth of July. She was telling everyone how horrible her fix-up date was. Everyone was laughing except one man in the back of the group.

When she was done with her tale, Gail asked her friend why she kept kicking her under the table while she was talking. She told her to come with her to the restroom.

Gail had no idea what she was going to hear. Her friend asked if she remembered what Mel looked like. She didn't. Then she told her that he was the guy who wasn't laughing while she was telling everyone what a jerk he was.

Gail was glad that she'd never mentioned his name, and hadn't stuck around long enough to run into him. She was out the door in a flash.

DRUNK

Danny was an attractive man of 58 with an average build and a good head of salt-and-pepper hair. He'd been divorced for six years. He went on maybe three dates a month and, like most men, was picky about who he dated.

The girls he went out with were from the Internet. He was cautious, as he had been burned several times by women who weren't who they said they were.

He felt he had much to offer the right woman. He had a good-paying job, lived in a great area, and had many interests. He never though he'd have this much trouble finding the right woman.

He knew he wasn't perfect, but nobody was. Everyone was flawed. It all depended on the flaw and how major it was.

Danny used to be built like a brick shithouse, but those days were long gone. Knowing this, he was aware that he was not going to find a middle-aged woman with the body of a 25-year-old.

He wasn't addicted to the Internet as most single people were. He would sit down about every other day and check out the dating site. He'd get maybe two or three messages, but nothing from anyone he was interested in.

One night while he was on the Internet, he received a short message from an attractive woman who said she was interested in communicating with him. At first he was curious, but then his juices started flowing, as he hardly ever received a message from someone he was physically attracted to.

He thought about it and decided to write her back, but didn't want to seem overly eager. He sent her a short reply, simply saying that he was also interested.

Her next message included her cell number and told him to call any evening after eight. That worked for him, as he would get home from work around 7:30.

He called her, and the first thing he asked was her name. They'd never mentioned their names in their communications.

Her name was Marsha, and she was a hair stylist. She was 52 and had never married. She said that she looked like her photos.

They had a good conversation, which lasted around 30 minutes. The usual volley of questions took about 15 minutes. This was the part that Danny hated; it was like a job interview over and over again.

They decided to meet for the first time at a Starbucks in a central location. Danny never took someone to dinner the first time they met.

Their date went well, and Danny asked her to go to dinner with him on Friday night. She passed his approval, which for him was a rare occurrence.

Seeing as they had met face to face, Danny asked if he could pick her up. Marsha seemed to like him, so she consented to having him pick her up at her house.

It was eight when he pulled into her neighborhood. It was a nice area with large houses. He thought that she must be doing well for herself.

He pulled into her driveway and noticed that her house was the smallest on the block. One thing he was not after was a woman who had money, as he had his own. If the woman had money, that would be a plus, but it was not necessary.

When Marsha opened her door, she was wearing an outfit that a 20-year-old should wear. She looked good, but a woman her age wearing a dress that short was not what he expected. He was a gentleman, and would never say anything bad about her choice of attire for the evening.

When he hugged her hello, he got a whiff of alcohol. He dismissed it, as he liked a drink after work, too.

He'd made reservations at an Italian restaurant that he liked. It was quaint and quiet, with great atmosphere. He liked to take his dates there, as the waiters all knew him and gave him great service.

They went to the bar to wait until their table was ready. He ordered a glass of red wine and she ordered a Long Island iced tea. He liked Long Islands too, but he was driving and they had an effect on him.

She had no trouble finishing her drink and, when the bartender asked if she wanted another, she said yes without blinking an eye.

Their table was ready and she brought her drink with her. Danny knew that if he'd had two Long Islands, he would be under the table. After that second drink, Danny noticed she was acting a little differently. She ordered a glass of red wine with her dinner and, as time went on, she was starting to slur her words. Danny was not enjoying himself because his date was getting drunk.

He should've cut her off, but didn't. After dinner, Danny asked for coffee and she asked for an after-dinner drink. That was the one that put her over the top.

She attempted to go to the ladies' room, but fell down after three steps. Danny was embarrassed, especially since the staff knew him. She was on the floor, with her short skirt up to her waist. Other customers were getting a show.

Like a gentleman, Danny helped her up and walked her to the restroom, where she disappeared. He waited for her until she came back out, and walked her back to the table. He knew right then that this was the last time he would see her.

He paid the check and helped her up as they walked to the front door. She was apologizing over and over for her behavior. Danny figured she'd been drinking before he arrived and then continued on their date.

He drove her back to her house, and when he pulled into the driveway, she was totally passed out. He wanted to get her out of his car before she puked. That would be the icing on the cake.

He actually did the fireman's carry to get her to the front door. He had to dig through her purse to find her house key. Once inside, he put her down on the couch, then turned and left as quickly as he could.

On his ride home, the only thing that really bothered him was how embarrassed he would be to go back to his favorite restaurant. He'd never been so embarrassed in his entire life.

IT ONLY TAKES ONE

Bart was an average-looking guy of 60. He'd been married for 25 years and had two grown sons. He was the owner of a CPA firm, and lived in a lovely condo overlooking the lake.

He dated about four times a month. Like most men, he was looking for the one woman who would make his socks go up and down. Most of his dates were one-and-dones. Sometimes, he felt that there was something wrong with him.

The computer was the only way he could find someone, as he didn't go into bars or nightclubs. Many times, he felt he'd spend the rest of his life by himself. His grown sons were married and had their own lives, and he never wanted to be a burden on them.

One day, a client of his called and asked if he'd like to meet a nice woman who also had a difficult time meeting someone. Bart asked the important questions, like how old, what's she look like, is she was divorced or widowed. The client didn't give him too much information; just told him they'd be a good match.

Bart was a little skeptical. The last time something similar happened, he was fixed up with someone who could pass for his mother. Shell-shocked was how described coming out of that experience.

After contemplating for a day or so, he decided to take a chance. After all, women weren't breaking down his door wanting to go out with him.

So, Bart called his client and expressed his interest in meeting her. Not seeing what she looked like really bothered him. He kept thinking about what happened last time.

He called her the same night he got her number. Her name was Geri and she had a young voice. When she answered the phone, he thought it was her daughter.

They had what he would call a very good conversation. They spent about an hour on the phone and found out they had much in common. They made plans for dinner the following Saturday night. She gave him directions to her home. The common denominator was that his client was her friend, so picking her up at her home wasn't an issue.

He was hoping that she looked as good as she sounded. He knew he was no Adonis, but he was a decent-looking man. He tried not to be too excited. That way if he was disappointed it wouldn't be as bad.

He arrived at her home about five minutes early, as he hated being late. He was holding his breath when he heard someone walking up to the door. He was greeted by a lovely smile worn by an attractive woman. She asked if he would like a glass of wine before they left. He said he would love one, so they sat and talked for about half an hour and then left.

He felt comfortable with her, and hoped she felt the same way. He knew it was a two-way street. His usual MO was that his date liked him but he didn't like her. This time, he liked her and hoped she liked him, too.

They enjoyed a wonderful dinner and conversation. When he took her home, she invited him in for coffee. He never wanted this night to end, as it had been a while since he'd felt so good about a date. If he had his way, they'd sit and talk for a few more hours.

They discussed how hard it was to meet someone who was on the same page. They talked about their bad dates and laughed about them. It was after midnight before he left. He asked to see her again, and she eagerly agreed. They kissed good-night and she closed the door. His drive home was like riding in the clouds.

They dated for six months and decided to move in with each other. They were married a year later, and today are totally happy.

The moral of this story is it only takes one to make the journey worthwhile.

EPILOGUE

What you have read are true stories from the single dating world. Just like those in *Check Please...& Hurry!*, these stories might be a litle hard to believe.

The single world is a tough place, as everyone has a story to tell, some good and some bad. More than 500 people have been interviewed between the two books, and the most interesting stories were selected for print.

The real names of the people in these stories have been changed for obvious reasons. Anyone who has been single and searching for the right match and his or her last date knows that the journey is not easy. Remember, it only takes one to make your journey successful.

Until your journey is completed, I'm sure you've been in the position to say, "Take My Date, Please!"

ABOUT THE AUTHOR

Richard W. Wiener is a retired high school athletic director who resides in Glenview, Illinois.

He has been a widower for six years, and is on his journey to find his last date. Having some really bad dates has inspired him to write this book.

He has written two other books:

Check Please...& Hurry!: Truthful Stories of Dates Gone Wrong and *I Have What??? One Man's Journey Through Breast Cancer*

Look for all his books at RichWiener.com or Amazon.com. You can follow Richard on Twitter @RichardWiener, and like each of his books on Facebook.

www.ingramcontent.com/pod-product-compliance
Lightning Source LLC
Chambersburg PA
CBHW052106070526
44584CB00017B/2366